How Political Leader's & People Can Develop Our Country

By MOHD RAFI

Student, Political Writer & Samaj Sevak

Preface

This book Gives knowledge about how to develop our country, How to end corruption , How to End Black Money, How to End Dowry, Rights of people, Rights to vote, Women's financial support for marriage and equality rights. I'm writing this book on my own which I wanted to do in my life for the humanity to bring awareness in our country people and all over the world. I wrote this book in the simple words of basic english which can be very easy to read and understand the concepts by any school student of 1st standard to bring awareness in all.

Contents

Chapter-1

1. How A Prime Minister Should Be :

- Prime Minister is a minister with super powers.

- Prime Minister should be honest and creative to the people and for our country. He has to be of clean image and shouldn't be money minded.

Coming To Prime Minister Duties & Responsibilities :

- Prime Minister is responsible to all state's security of our country.

- Prime minister have to make sure all state Chief ministers, Cabinet ministers, MP & MLA's are working towards their state development. All state chief ministers have to report prime minister on daily and weekly basis to ensure that work is going on smoothly in an efficient way.

- Prime minister is responsible to boost economy and Gdp Growth. To boost economy of our country prime minister have to believe in dialogue and professional relationship with all over the world including neighbor countries. Trade is the best option for any country to earn money. So we have to believe in dialogue and maintaining a good relationship with all over the world is necessary because we don't know exactly how much we can earn from which country by trade. So it is important for us to maintain and keep improving in developing trade with all countries.

- Two Countries who are nuclear powers can't fight with each other because it's impossible to fight. Even if both the countries starts fighting with each other that's not a fight that will be a war which is a nuclear war. So its not possible to fight, only the option is peace dialogue between the two countries.

- Prime minister is responsible if any soldier martyrs because two neighbor countries prime minister perceptions are different and unequal.

- Prime minister have to be very calm and polite, he has to believe in dialogue not in war. Prime minister have a huge responsibility of people's if one decision have taken wrong by prime minister that will effect to crores of people of our country who are going to suffer from it.

- Prime minister have to be very careful while taking any decision, he has to check and confirm whether the decision which he is going to take is right or wrong and shouldn't effect to any particular religion or community.

- PM is overall responsible to maintain law & order in our country, his work is only to take proper and correct decisions. Rest of the work will be take care by our selective ministers.

- If Prime minister is honest, want to do something for our country then in few months people can see the changes in their states & cities. He has to work on initiating employment for youth instead of wasting time and money on Foreign tours, Advertising, Media, Statues and in waste projects. In this precious time if he focus to initiate employment then our country youth can easily get jobs and our country itself move towards development.

- PM have to do press conferences, have to answer to public and media for their questions which arising in their minds. People and media have the rights to ask questions to prime minister as well as they have the rights to receive answers from our prime minister.

- If Prime minister really wants to develop our country then law & order towards development can be pass within a day. If any project is good for the people then no one will oppose to it ruling party have full powers to pass the development projects.

- The main and important point is prime minister is voted to power to listen to our country people not to listen to his own thoughts.

Chapter-2

2.How A Chief Minister Should be :

- Chief Minister is a minister with second (2^{Nd}) Super power.
- If Chief minister is honest towards his work and development then no one can stop him . After Prime minister, Chief minister have the powers to develop their states. CM can take any steps towards development of their state and can implement it in just few minutes.

Coming To Chief Minister Duties and Responsibilities :

- The main point in between Prime minister and chief minister is their both work is same. PM works for our country and CM for their state.

- Public selected their prime minister and chief minister to serve them, listen to them, but as a fact what they are doing now is sharing their own thoughts with people. PM and CM have to be keep in mind very clearly that they have been selected and voted to power to listen to their country people.

- As I said even chief minister have the same responsibility like prime minister to maintain law & order, safety of people, keeping the state safe etc.

- CM have to check daily, weekly and monthly report of his state towards their state development projects.

- Chief minister is also responsible to bring funds and investments for their state development by central government to fund their state projects towards the development of their concerned state. He can also bring foreign investments in his state by trying his best.

- CM have to check & confirm that all his ministers are working for welfare of the people, for the people, as a servant of the people or not.

- The Prime minister, Chief minister and state ministers have powers but actually they are the public servants. They are voted to power to serve people not for their own comforts and luxury life. They have to listen to people, listen to their problems and then they have to solve that problems which are facing by public.

- Now ministers are not giving value to their country people who they voted him to power, they are not listening to public , now ministers are coming live in their selective media and sharing their own thoughts with public and get disappeared.

- This have to be stop, they have to work for the people, they have to listen to their people and also they have to serve to the people.

Chapter -3

3.How To End Corruption & Black Money :

- This part is a game changer to develop any country.

- To develop any country the first thing leaders have to do is ending corruption & black money from our country. This part plays an important role in developing any country.

Factors to End Corruption From :

1.Corrupted Leaders &

2.Corrupted Government Officers

- The first Point to end corruption from leaders & government officers are starting Electronic digital payments. The payments which are electronic, AEPS, Bank Transfer, Card Payments, online payments etc., except cash transactions.

- When any leader or government officer comes to power or joins a government job, that leader or government officer have to provide all his assets, investments, bank accounts details , savings etc., including their all family members father, mother, spouse, children, brother & sisters. So if government trackers have these all details of leaders and government officers they will keep tracking to them regularly then its easy to catch them. If they receive any credits or deposits in their accounts, if they suddenly gets rich & property holders doubled than the given details by wrong track or something that will help government tracking officers to catch them easily. They have to answer for every credits and deposits in their accounts.

- Those who are receiving credits and deposits in their bank accounts other than their salary needs to be answer for their credits.

- To end corruption cash transactions has to be stop completely or allowing only 1000/-Rs.(One Thousand rupees) of cash from banks per month per member every month for emergency need of cash.

- The overall solution to end corruption is by stopping using of cash and starting to pay by digital electronic payments. So that will have data of every person in our country about what he does, where he is working and how much he is earning daily, monthly and yearly. So by implementing these things we can end corruption upto 99% .

What is Black Money :

- Black money is that which a business person or businessmen doesn't paid tax of his business earnings and sold his product or service illegally without recording that business transaction in their computer billing system is known as Black Money.

- The same way customers or people who buys something and paid money without a computerized bill to save tax money of their purchases will give chance to that businessmen or consumer to store that total transaction money in their pockets as black money. What will happens if this continues in future is government will face a budget and income shortage problem for their uses for which they have to increase the product & services costs which will directly impact to the public only. Like this the cost of living becomes expensive in our daily life and also in our our whole country.

- To avoid this, people who are purchasing or buying something ask that service provider or business shop persons to give computer generated bill for your purchases while paying them and payments have do be done by your debit/credit card or use electronic and digital payments. Which gives data to the government to collect tax from that particular business persons of his business earnings. By asking computer generated bill and paying a little bit tax on your purchases by electronic payment, you're asking that business person to pay tax on his business earnings Which will not only help the government to earn tax income even you're helping yourself to decrease the cost of living in your daily life.

- The tax money which you paid at the time of your purchases will get back to you by getting double in the future as in the form of your earning income government returns to you which people doesn't understand this concept easily.

- Black money can only be stop by using Digital & Electronic payments completely. To stop Corruption & black money Use of cash need to be stop completely.

- By Stopping cash transactions completely, starting use of electronic and digital payments only the solution to end corruption & Black money in our country.

  Note : This will be useful to any countries in the world who are facing corruption and black money problems in their countries.

Chapter-4

4. How to Develop our Country :

- The first and very important factor to develop our country is by initiating employment or creating jobs. If our ministers focus to initiate employment then development itself starts automatically. Employment is the very big concern nowadays, if youth are unemployed then our country becomes weak and poor. If this problem continues then it becomes very hard to develop our country. So to develop any country they have to give importance to Skill, Education and employment of youth. So to initiate employment government needs to use lateral thinking by going beyond the creative approach. For example cloud computing which create jobs by itself cloud computing is the job creator for himself and for others. So government needs to learn this thing by going beyond everything for job creation.

How to implement government projects :

- To implement Government project and how to make it successful these are the things that government have to focus on it.

- Starting a project from Prime minister then goes to their selective department minister. From there to the state ministers, MP's and MLA's.

When a project starts how it goes I'll show you below

- Prime Minister-> Department Selective Minister -> State Minister-> MP's ->MLA's->MLC and councilor or corporator.
- What is happening here is i'll explain you exactly right away. After the project starts till it reaches to public few ministers, government officers and their relatives ate everything totally for only to show record they will give that benefit to few of the people who are working for them at the election time.

- MLA's, MLC, Councilor or corporator (Street Leader or Ward Leaders) plays an important role in between public to serve them and listen to them.
- Public believes to their area MLA or city leader that he will do something for them but whichever the project starts it will not benefit to the common people. Why this happens everyone knows that and I have already explained this above.
- So to stop this, government needs to bring new steps to benefit to people from their projects.

- Leaders have to be honest with their area peoples. Chief minister have to check every projects with 100% accuracy by keeping an eye and tracking their ministers, the project started is benefiting people or not by their selected ministers of their areas.

- Chief Minister and MLA's needs to hire employees to serve and help people under each and every single area of their constituency.

- Suppose if under one constituency it consists of 10 local areas then that is the responsibility of their ruling party and MLA to setup 10 offices, 10 employees in that 10 local areas under that one constituency to serve people and solve their problems immediately, they have to be available daily, recording public problems daily, the same updating with their MLA and solving their problem within 24 hours.

- So if any political party follow these steps and start serving to people like this then the people get benefited by every projects which government starts. Then our country people will live happily and peacefully without any problem.

- To complete any project Chief minister have to be sincere and have to track their ministers, keep an eye on their ministers also on their project works.

Chapter-5

5.Foreign Investments in Our Country :

- Foreign investments plays an important role to develop our country. When foreign or Multi National companies comes to our country they will also bring employment, money and tax for our country. When they come here they will initiate employment which our people needs and also pays tax which helps our government to raise their income as well as with that tax money our government can initiate employment for our country people. So overall foreign companies going to benefit our country and our government needs to bring them in our country right. So how it is possible I'm going to explain you here.

Important Factors to bring Foreign Investments :

- Our Leaders, Government officers and our country people who are well versed with their power and knowledge overseas as well as in our country, can bring foreign investments by promoting our country peoples talent. How to attract foreign investors is by giving them special status, Free Business Registration License, Foreign Minister Support, Government officers support, Free Electricity & Tax Exemption for one year or till the company gets into profit.

- As we have 100% FDI (Foreign Direct Investment) in our country except few sectors so it is very easy for foreign companies to invest in our country and will provide full government support to foreign companies at 0% (Zero Percent) Corruption rate.

- These are the important factors to bring foreign investments in our country. I request to our government as well as our country peoples who are in power overseas try their best to bring foreign investors by promoting our governments full support of giving special status, Free Business Registration license, Free support of foreign minister, Free support of government officers, Tax exemption and free Electricity to

foreign companies till one year or till the
company gets into profit.

Chapter-6

6. How to Serve Our Country People :

- This is the important part from the whole book
  for   our country people.

- Our Country People are the real owners and
  leaders are the tenants but after the elections
  political leaders get disappeared. When they
  come to power they ignore & forget all their
  promises which they made before the elections.

- I request to our leaders and common peoples of
  our country don't forget anything which you
  promised to public at the time of election. Keep
  in mind that people are not fools to forget what
  you have promised. Fulfill your promises which
  you made before the elections if you fulfilled
  your promises which you made then in the next

elections you don't need to ask people to vote people themselves will vote to you this is honesty of our country people.

- Treat people as your boss, serve them as they are the owners(People) and you're the tenants (Leader) then people loves you, trust you as well as without any doubt they vote you.

Chapter-7

7. Rights of People :

- I and we are the citizens of this country and everyone is equal citizens of this country either he is Hindu, Muslim, Sikh, Isaayi, Jain, Dalit, Budh etc., our constitution have given equal rights to all people of our country there is no discrimination in religions.
- I and we the people of our country have the full rights to know that what our country ministers , state ministers and city ministers are doing, what they are working for after becoming a leader of our country, state and cities. Presently Which work they are doing for our city and streets, how

much central government sanctioned fund to our state ministers for our state and city developments. Each and every single rupee which is sanctioned by the government to our state developments our state people have the full rights to know for our record that what our government is doing for us whether the fund given to our city ministers have been used for public welfare and city development or not.

- I and we the people of our country have full rights to know how much our country is earning per day per month and per year from our tax money, Bonds, investments, Properties, Rents, Services etc., Educated people who know this things have to bring awareness in people this is very important for the people to know.

- After 70 years of independence also we are facing problems of Corruption, Black Money, Scams, Terrors, Riots etc., in our country. To stop this things people of our country needs to know online as well as offline by daily, weekly and monthly with full details of government income from all sources like assets, services , Rents, taxes etc., there is nothing to hide from people in the name of secrecy where comes to spending of money by government.

- We as a responsible people of our country wants to know where our country and state ministers are spending our tax money. We have the full rights to know even if it is about a single rupee of tax money. There is no secrecy should be used in the name of money already we are facing this problem since 70 years because of this secrecy but not anymore. The name secrecy betrayed our country people with scams, corruption, black money etc.,

- We the people of our country really wants to know and have full rights to know how much money our government is spending in different projects, what it benefits to the people and how.

- Now people of our country have changed themselves even they want to know every single step, information as well as government work details that how government is working for public welfares.

- I request to our country people that bring awareness in yourself. Whenever any leader comes to you at the time of election ask him to release their manifesto or work details which he is going to do give it in writing by signing on it. This is the time which we can't believe to anyone then how can we believe on that leader who is in power. People have to keep asking questions to their leaders till he completes that work if people don't ask him about what he is doing to them till that time he won't do anything for your city.

- Some leaders after giving in writing also after the election if someone asks to them again they will give excuses like this that I did my work what I've promised but I think we got a little problem while doing the work in this city etc., don't leave them until they fulfill your promises keep asking questions like ask him to give details where he did his work ,when he did, which work he did, when he completed his work there and when he is going to start work in your city.

- The important rights of people are to know exactly where our tax money, revenues, bonds, gains through which government is earning and where it is using by our government in which way for what purpose they are using it there. What it benefit to people and how. People have to ask government to show all their money spending, expenses, incomes etc., by online daily, weekly and monthly. There is no need to maintain any secrecy in the name of money when it comes to money expenditure.

- People have to also check for government tenders to whom government is giving every contracts or tenders. Because when they come to power they use to give government tenders to their relatives, friends, or to people who knows them. What actually happening here is they are giving tenders for themselves in the name of their friends and relatives. So peoples also have the right of responsibility to keep tracking it they finds something wrong.

- These are all rights of the people to avoid Scams, Black money and corruption from the ministers.
- Everyone who is reading this book please share this things with your family and friends who are not aware of it.

Chapter-8

8.End of Dowry System :

- People already knows that dowry is illegal in our country and also in the world.
- In our country already government banned dowry and declared it as illegal as per the dowry act 1961. Even that people are paying dowry to the groom's family, why they are paying it do they have more money to pay dowry or is that the failure of government law or what. Actually this is the failure of government, law is on the correct way but government is not acting properly on this law.

- Those who belongs to rich family they don't have any problem to pay dowry but those who belongs to poor family are suffering from this act of paying dowry by rich peoples. Because of this dowry poor people are suffering too much even after law is there in our country but still people are looking for dowry from bride's family. Poor people are any how arranging dowry by thinking and in tension of their daughter's marriage. This is becoming huge tension for people, at the time of marriage anyhow they are arranging dowry for their daughter but later they are suffering too much because of this dowry.This needs to be stop, bring awareness in people that if anyone is asking for dowry then immediately raise a complaint to police about them. If all people of our country act accordingly by law of dowry by warning them who are asking and looking for dowry then automatically dowry will stop by itself. Our country people lives happily if all people help each other warn them when this dowry seekers comes in front of you.

- Note : This have to be bring in notice of our government to act strictly and make it active this law accordingly.

9. Bring a law ordinance of financial support to Bride's family at the time of marriage :

- This is the law which change our country totally with this each and every people of our country lives happily. If this law ordinance passes in our country then people of our country don't bother for their daughter's marriage .

- Government have to bring a law for financial support to bride's family by groom and government including their state ministers. Groom have to give the financial support of minimum 1,00,000/-Rs. (One lakh rupees) to bride's family for marriage expenses and government have to give the financial support of minimum 50,000/-Rs. (Fifty thousand rupees) to bride's family for marriage expenses at the time of bride's marriage . Money will be credited to bride's account 15 days before to marriage.

- Note : This law ordinance have to be bring in notice in parliament. Government have to pass this Law.

Chapter-10

10.Bring a Law ordinance for women's support to her parents after her marriage by herself :

- What this law benefits to women and how? I'm going to explain you right here.

- Most of the parents have only one daughter or few have two daughters and they don't have any son or if they have any son he is not ready to take responsibility of their parents. Then they have is only daughter who is ready to take responsibility of their parents even after her marriage but she will the face problem from her husband or from her law family. That person can be of anyone we can't disclose it exactly.

- Women's are equal to the men's they have full rights to support her parents and family for a lifetime even after her marriage there is nothing to do with her law family this is none of their business. She can do any business or job in which she is comfortable to support their family.

- Note : This law ordinance have to be bring in notice in parliament. Government have to pass this Law.

Chapter-11

11.Public Power or Common People's Power (Vote)

- Now Leaders are not fulfilling their promises they will just come before the election and say we are doing this, we are doing that but finally they don't have any valid proof to show what they did.

- We are the people who believes them blindly. Each and every single people of our country and state make sure you know that what they did to you, what they did to your area after coming to power. Keep in mind those things ask your leader to prove what he did give you in writing and also ask him to give in writing what he is going to do, in how many days he is going to complete it.

- Don't trust a political leader because they will only say in the speech but they don't fulfill their promises completely. So we have to keep asking questions till they complete their work which he promises.

- Ask your leader daily and weekly what he did till now, how much government sanctioned fund to develop our city. Ask your leader to be available for you daily in your city to serve the people by keeping his office and employees in your each local areas to listen to us , to solve our problems, to develop our local area , find people needs etc.,

- Don't vote them who are money minded choose to correct person in your city as your leader who is honest and who treats you as his boss. Think and vote to the honest leader in the name of development , employment , house schemes , who treats you as your boss, who listens to you etc.,

- Don't vote them if someone ask you to vote in the name of religion, temples, mosques, churchs and in the name of any traditional things which is not going to benefit you. They will do anything to cast vote in their pockets in the name of religion , creating hatred between the religions etc., If this kind of leaders don't know how to develop our country they will divide our country people in the name of religion to cast your vote in their pockets. Be aware of this things and don't waste your 5 years by giving your vote to this kind of leaders.
- Public power is only vote which comes to you only one time in 5 years so think and choose correct leader to vote.

- Don't Trust any leader blindly, use your mind, think better and vote.

Thanking You All

✓ If you really find my knowledge useful to you then share with your friends about this things and bring awareness in them. Please write me a mail in the below mentioned Email address if you like my book.

✓ Email : starconsultant21@Gmail.com
✓ Follow me on my 'How to develop our country' Facebook page and you can Buy other Books from my facebook page.

✓ I'll be back with my next book soon Thankyou.